Do It All?

Understanding God's Plan, Purpose and
Positioning for You as a
Kingdom Multi-Hyphenate

By Randi J. Norman

Cover Design: Mantle Branding, LLC.

Cover Photo Credits:
Abigail Medina
Forbes Visuals
Charlotte Rhymes

Editor: NJ Kingdom Enterprises, LLC.
www.njkingdomenterprises.com

Dedication

To my Sweet Girl, Leila and my Buddy, aka Trey Trey, Gary III, who are Kingdom Multi-hyphenates in their own right. May you lean into all that God has created you to be for His glory.

To my Love, Gary II, for always allowing me to fly, as high and free as God leads me, as the kite to your string. I love you!

To My Daddy, who gave me Jesus. I love and miss you!

Acknowledgment

I would not be who I am or where I am without two very important people. Almost 20 years ago, in 2005, I passed a billboard on I-4 in Tampa, FL, for a church called Revealing Truth Ministries. My life hasn't been the same since. Pastor Greg Powe and Pastor Deborah Powe have both made a mark on my life that can never be erased. They fostered a safe environment for me to learn, grow, develop, and stretch beyond my perceived capacity by teaching the simple truth that is the Word of God! Thank you!

When I heard the Holy Spirit instruct me to write this book, He also told me that I couldn't do it all myself. He showed me one person: Mrs. Neysa Jones. Thank you for taking action immediately and responding with the same sense of urgency I felt from the Lord! I could not have completed this project without your guidance. Another Book Baby has been born! Thank you!

When it came time to design the cover, I initially thought I'd do it myself. However, the Lord told me no. I had to ask for help from my community of creatives again. This time, I asked the Brandmaster himself, Mike Bigos! Thank you,

Mike, for showing up for me on short notice before your big trip. It means more to me than you'll ever know. Your gift as a prophetic designer is undeniable.

Finally, I want to thank my Senior Pastor, Bryan Powe. The time we have spent together over the years has meant the world to me. Our conversations are rarely brief and always filled with such rich wisdom, mutual sharpening, and sound counsel. Thank you for always listening and walking alongside me on this journey! We'll keep walking until we see what God said!

Foreword

As Pastor Bryan Powe, the Lead Pastor and Servant at Revealing Truth Ministries, I have had the privilege of dedicating over two decades to collaborating with some of the most inspired creative minds in the body of Christ. Our mission has been to capture and express God's love through every artistic medium possible, showing "How wide, how long, how high, and how deep" His love truly is. It is in this determined community of faith and creativity that I have had the joy of working alongside Randi J. Norman, a truly dedicated servant of God and a co-laboring creative with a heart passionately attuned to God's spirit.

Randi J. is an individual whose strengths are profound and spiritually rooted. Her availability to serve, sensitivity to the Spirit of God, willingness to give her all and courage to forge paths where others might hesitate are qualities that not only define her character, but also empower her life. Whether leading by example or supporting behind the scenes, Randi has consistently been where God calls her to be. Through her relentless "Yes" to God, she has embraced the uncharted year after year, assignment after assignment.

This book, a reflective and transformative exploration of one's relationship with God, is a testament to Randi's depth as a student and follower of Christ. It promises not only to walk you through the activation of your gifts, but to deepen your understanding of who God is and who you are in Him. Her insights foster an absolute attitude where life revolves around the glory of God, reflecting His multidimensional nature.

Randi's gift of storytelling, her life's experiences, and her spiritual gifts serve as the backdrop throughout the pages of this vital work. Her motivation stems from witnessing many wander, lost within the Kingdom, uncertain of their calling and identity. Her response, this book, aims to simplify the complex, ensuring that one's unique calling is easily understood without diluting its essence.

Writing this foreword was not merely an honor; it was a life-giving experience. Having felt the weight of being called but misunderstood, I relate deeply to the themes within this book. Randi's words have brought peace to my soul, and I am confident they will bring peace to yours as well. Prepare to embark on a journey that will clarify, challenge, and cultivate your walk with God like never before.

~ Pastor Bryan Powe, Lead Pastor and Servant, Revealing Truth Ministries

Table of Contents

Dedication iii

Acknowledgment iv

Foreword vi

Introduction 1

SECTION 1: EDUCATE 7

    Chapter 1 - WHAT: Become All Things to All Men 9

    Chapter 2 - WHY: Why Me? 17

SECTION 2: CONSECRATE 22

    Chapter 3 - PURPOSE 24

    Chapter 4 - USE THEM WELL 29

SECTION 3: DEMONSTRATE 38

    Chapter 5 - WHEN: Can I Do It All Now? 40

    Chapter 6 - WHERE: Same Cup, Different Audience 56

    Chapter 7 - WHO: A Who, Not A What 65

Conclusion 71

About the Author 76

Notes 77

Introduction

Imagine the scene: you're at a networking event. The room is full of people milling about one another. Some are getting a bite to eat. Others are chatting. You see people exchanging social niceties along with social media handles. There's equal parts laughter and nervous energy wafting through the air. After all, most of us are meeting one another for the first time. The rest of us don't really know each other. And none of us, while fans of dogs and ponies, are interested in being a part of either show. We're all here for the same reason: to meet new people and connect; however, most of us are still quite nervous. You can feel it in the air. It's palpable.

Now, it's time to make introductions.

"So, tell us a little about you and what you do."

Really? That's where we're starting? I mean, that's where all of these introductory conversations start, right? It always starts at the place where I feel stuck. It always starts where I have no idea where to actually start. It always starts at the same gate that I know is gonna be stuck before I even enter the race.

I have no idea how to answer that question!

1

Who am I and what do I do?

For a long time, this question had my palms sweating and my heart racing. I had no idea how to answer it. It seemed like such a simple question, yet it was LOADED for me. My creative resume has SECTIONS. On any given day, for any given event, I could be found showing up as a:

- Host/Emcee
- Author
- Singer
- Director
- Spoken Word Poet
- Actor
- Model
- Designer
- Speaker
- Zumba Instructor
- Event Planner

I am what has become known as a multi-hyphenate.

Multi-hyphenate:

Someone who does several different jobs,

especially in the entertainment industry.

("Multi-hyphenate")[1]

At first, when I'd be in a room similar to the one described, I'd approach it like one of those origami paper fortune teller games the kids used to make back in the day. Or like a game of ini-mini-miney-moe. Depending on the room I was in, I'd feel like I had to pick an option. Am I a singer today? A poet? A writer? A designer? An event planner? A host? Who do I say that I am…today? What do I say that I do? Will I tell them my profession…at the moment? Will I tell them something more aligned with the expectations of the room? All the while, in my head, I see my fingers slip inside the four corners of the carefully folded paper game of choice and begin to move them in and out as I internally recite, "Which one will I choose today?" in a little sing-songy voice.

See, while being a multi-hyphenate in the entertainment industry is accepted, lauded and applauded, **it's often not seen quite the same way in traditional ministry.** If you sing, you sing. If you usher, you usher. If you preach, you preach. If you park cars, you park cars. If you go to the prisons, you go to prisons. If you're a nurse, you're a nurse. If you play keys, you play keys. The expectation is that you only move from spot to spot to spot to find your spot… and then you **stay there.** That is your spot. We see it all of the time. People serve in ministry, at the same ministry, in the same position for 30 years, never having explored other areas of ministry, much like going to work, aiming for the coveted gold watch at retirement. They settle into the routine of the assignment and plant. They become known as that thing, and it becomes a part of their identity. "You know, Deacon So-and-So, who parks the cars." or "Yeah, Sis So-and-So, who sings in the choir." So much so that others don't know, nor does "So-and-So" even know who they are outside of it.

Not only do I believe we are capable of so much more, but I believe you, reading this book, know it, too. I believe that you know that you are as multidimensional as the God you serve. Maybe you are the one who has been serving in the same place and operating in a singular gift for many years, and you desire more. Maybe you're already flowing in multiple gifts, but have trouble explaining how you move to others, and really understanding it yourself. Maybe you are somewhere in between. Either way, I believe God wants us to go on this journey together. He wants us to dive into the fundamentals of being a Kingdom Multi-hyphenate and why your assignment is important. He wants us to understand His plan, purpose, and positioning for us as a Kingdom Multi-hyphenate. And, He wants us to grab ahold of this **NOW.**

Whatever You Want, God

This very simple four-word prayer has caused my life to be very "interesting." We tend to use "interesting" when we don't really know what to call a thing. It's not good or bad, just "interesting". "Whatever you want, God" has been my prayer for years. It was all that would spring forth from my belly when I would talk to God about my life and what He'd have me to do. All that would come up for me was, "Whatever you want, God." My husband would often tease me about it and tell me to be more specific with God. But the truth is, I didn't and still don't have anything else to say. It truly is my heart's desire to be used by God however He sees fit. That has been my heart's desire ever since I was a little girl at Joint Heirs Christian Center in Jacksonville, FL.

From the day I saw my daddy give his life to Christ and get filled with the Holy Spirit, I knew I wanted God to do whatever He wanted with my life. At the age of 9, I gave my life to Christ, and He really has had my heart for 35 years. Oh, what a time we have had! It has been full of surrender and discomfort and mistakes and forgiveness. It has been scary and exhilarating and fun and nerve-racking. It has been "interesting." But, I wouldn't trade it for anything because, as the old folks say, I know too much about Him; you can't make me doubt Him. Those 35 years have been a journey of **learning more** of Him (educate), discovering and accepting who I am in Him (consecrate), and understanding how to put feet to my faith because of Him (demonstrate). They have been a time of **Education, Consecration and Demonstration.** This is the journey we'll embark on throughout these pages.

My assignment for this book is to dive into the process, as God has shown me, of understanding His plan, purpose, and positioning for you and me as a Kingdom Multi-hyphenate. I will share some of the pivotal moments along my journey with God and the things He revealed to me. I hope that you will learn from them and courageously embrace all that He is asking of you. When given this assignment, the Lord placed a sense of urgency in my Spirit. He said **NOW,** so I know there is someone who needs to know what He has shown me **NOW.** My prayer is that as you read, you too, would begin to open yourself up to whatever God wants to do in and through you with confidence, wisdom, and understanding **NOW.**

SECTION 1: EDUCATE

Learning More of Him and Discovering Who You Are in Him

"What are you doing, God?" and "Why me?" These are the two questions I always ask myself when God decides to take me on some new adventure. I didn't realize it initially, but it has been the Holy Spirit's way of guiding me to seek intellectual, moral, and social instruction from Him.

Educate:

To give intellectual, moral, and social instruction to someone.

("Educate")[2]

I needed to care about what God cared about and be curious about why He was asking me to get involved in what He was doing. God has had to educate me on who He is, what I am, and why He has called me, of all people. He has made me rewrite what I thought I knew about myself. He has had to renew my mindset regarding how I saw myself while helping me understand why it is necessary to see things differently. This will be your work. It is the necessary work of a Kingdom Multi-hyphenate.

Chapter 1 - WHAT: Become All Things to All Men

The word **"What"** is defined as specifying the identity, nature, or value of something. When we know what a thing is, we can categorize it. When we know how to define a thing, we know what to do with it. We know which box to check or which box to put it in. The problem with being a multi-hyphenate is that **we don't fit nicely into any box**. Standardization doesn't quite work. But what if the problem wasn't really the problem? What if the problem wasn't that we don't fit nicely into the box? What if the real problem was how we saw not fitting into the box? What if the real problem was that we thought we were supposed to fit into some box created by someone who was trying to fit in themselves? What if the real problem is more about how we perceive ourselves, rather than how others see us?

So many of us are gifted in so many areas, but we force ourselves to pick a lane or choose a gift to walk in. We force ourselves to decide which field or stage we want to play on. We force ourselves to go down a path and stay there.

To be called a "jack of all trades and a master of none" was not a good thing growing up. It was a way for people to label you as unfocused, indecisive, or flighty. When you heard that saying pointed at someone, you already knew they were low-key throwing shade, i.e. making a subtle insult.

Everywhere we go, from the time we are little, we are asked to choose. Everything is "this or that". Do you like white meat or dark meat? Is your favorite color red or blue? Do you want a boy or a girl? Are you a cat person or a dog person? Are you an extrovert or an introvert? Do you like sweet snacks or salty snacks? There are categories everywhere!

Now, don't get me wrong, choosing is important. My daddy used to always say, "Life is choice-driven; choose wisely!" And the bible tells us to choose ye this day whom you will serve. There are some things that require choice. Those things tend to be about choosing Christ, not about choosing how we operate in Christ. That's not really up to us, right? Not if we are to be spirit-led.

On the surface, choosing to be a dog person or a cat person, or an animal person at all doesn't really seem like a big deal until it is. Until you've checked DOG and you've argued that

DOG is the only way, and you've built your life around choosing DOG, and now, God is telling you to get a CAT. Wait...what, God? See, this is the moment when panic sets in. It's the moment when we typically dig our heels in and say, NO! I don't do CATS! They smell, and they pee all over the place, and that whole back arch thing is just creepy. We start going down the list of why we don't do CATS.

God didn't ask you any of that. He said go get the cat.

What you don't know is that you are about to receive a call from the adoption agency you and your husband have been working with. The little girl who needs a family loves cats. God is preparing you for what is about to happen. He is preparing you for someone you are about to meet. He is preparing you to answer a prayer that she prayed in her secret place at night just before bedtime where no one else could hear. He is preparing you to be a demonstration to her that God is with her, hears her, and cares about her - even her desire to have a CAT.

You don't know that, though, so you continue to wrestle - DOG OR CAT?

What if you chose AND instead of OR?

Something that seemed so trivial, so insignificant, like a personal choice, was really a sneaky way the enemy has begun to pervert our thoughts.

To pervert is simply to alter from its original course, meaning, or state to a distortion or corruption of what was first intended. You see, the enemy cannot create, he can only resort to distortion. He took the power that God gave us to choose and distorted it so that we would become so locked into a seemingly menial choice that we became inflexible with God.

1 Corinthians 9:22 (KJV) tells us that Paul became all things to all men so that some may be saved. This scripture came alive in my life when I was forced by God to go to the drama ministry. Yes…forced. I know that sounds strong, but God set me up. I was salty about it back then, but I get it now. He had no other choice but to set me up. I wanted no part of it! I was petrified of the stage. I didn't want to act. I had no desire at all. Yes, I know I heard the Lord. As a matter of fact, I actually had a vision from God. That's the best way I can explain it. I heard the Lord say join the drama ministry.

I then ran down a list to God of things I don't do:

I don't act.

I don't do public speaking.

I don't like the stage.

I don't want to be in the front.

I told God who I am:

I'm a background player.

I'm a supporting team member.

I'm an introvert.

Then came the vision. God showed me running into the Drama Ministry director and exactly how our interaction would unfold:

"So, Randi, when are you coming to drama practice?"

"When is it?"

"Monday night."

"I'll be there Monday."

The end.

No way was that happening. I avoided her like the plague. When I saw her coming, I went the other way. It worked, until it didn't. I literally almost accidentally ran into her. And guess what? The conversation went exactly as I had seen it in my vision.

"So, Randi, when are you coming to drama practice?"

"When is it?"

"Monday night."

"I'll be there Monday."

The end.

On day one, our foundational scripture was shared with me:

For though I be free from all men, yet have I made myself servant unto all, that I might gain the more. And unto the Jews I became as a Jew, that I might gain the Jews; to them that are under the law, as under the law, that I might gain them that are under the law; to them that are without law, as without law, (being not without law to God, but under the law to Christ,) that I might gain them that are without law. To the weak became I as weak, that I might gain the weak: **I am made all things to all men, that I might by all means save some.** ~**1 Corinthians 9:19-22 (KJV)**

I didn't know then that this would become the foundational scripture for my life.

In Drama Ministry, we become various characters to tell the story of Christ and draw people to Him. We use laughter, exaggeration, and real-life situations to illustrate the Word of God. This allows the audience to see themselves reflected in the stories and understand how God moved, protected, guided, and cared for the characters on stage, just as He does for us in real life. I learned to become something other than Randi. The only instruction from my director was to trust the Holy Spirit. She only required that we ask Him how to become that character. She would ask, "What did the Holy Ghost say?" She didn't want to know what you thought it should be or what you were afraid to try or what you saw someone else do. She only wanted to know what the Holy Ghost said to you about becoming this thing.

I had chosen BACKGROUND. I was good at BACKGROUND. I am a great planner and team member for any project. But God was requiring that I choose FOREGROUND too. He wanted me to learn to become anything to tell His story.

And this is the point.

What am I? Simply put, I'm a storyteller - created to use my life and every gift He gives me to tell His story for His glory.

No longer do I feel compelled to be this OR that. I embrace a life of AND. I am this AND that. I am poet **and** actor and singer **and** model **and** planner **and** organizer **and** director and designer **and** leader **and** BGV **and** author **and** host. I am whoever He needs me to be so that someone can see Him and know that He loves them.

And you are too!

You are as multifaceted as the brilliant God you serve. You can boldly check as many boxes as He chooses to place you in. For we must not forget that the jack-of-all-trades quote that we hear so often is usually left in an incomplete state.

"A jack-of-all- all trades is a master of none, but oftentimes is better than a master of one." (Common Proverb, attributed to William Shakespeare)[3]

Oh, and it was actually meant as a compliment. Imagine that.

Chapter 2 - WHY: Why Me?

Pastor Powe, the founding Pastor of my church, Revealing Truth Ministries would say, "God doesn't need your ability, He needs your availability."

The Bible tells us that God has a plan for us. He does. His plan is to do us good and see us face-to-face in heaven for eternity. That's the end goal. Everything else is in between. It's the middle or waiting period, which we'll talk about a little later.

Take Adam and Eve for example. God's plan was for them to dwell with Him and commune with Him, continuously. He desired an eternal, uninterrupted connection with them, where they marveled at Him and His creation, obeyed His Word, and had faith in Him. Now, if God is sovereign, which He is, and if God is omnipotent, which He is, and if God is perfect in all of His ways, which He is, then one decision by the thing HE MADE cannot change the end goal of His plan. A suggestion from a fallen angelic being, Lucifer, cannot have the power to alter all that God intended. The middle? Well, by giving us free will, is always up for debate.

Why me? This question is, at least for me, not a question about cause, reason, or purpose, which is typically what we're after when we ask 'why.' We want to know why something happened or why something is. We want to know the purpose of a thing. 'Why me?' is typically not really a question at all; it's more questioning. It's more in line with unbelief. It's more adjacent to disagreement with God. It really is a question about worthiness, and the truth is, I'm not the first to wrestle with that question. You're not the first to wrestle with that question either.

In **Psalms 8:4 (NKJV),** David writes, *"What are mere mortals that you should think about them, human beings that you should care for them?"* David was wrestling with the question of worthiness. We, like the King James Version, often ask the same question: *Who am I that you are mindful of me? Who am I that you would make me a little lower than God?* **(KJV)** We often struggle with seeing ourselves as worthy to be thought of by God, let alone used by Him.

Worthy is defined as having worth or value. Webster defines worth as moral or personal value; the value of something measured by its qualities OR by the esteem in which it is held OR the equivalent of a specified amount. In other words, worth is determined by what one party is specifically willing to give in exchange for something of the other party's. God was willing to give His Son, Jesus, in exchange for you. God decided that your value was far above rubies. He decided that you are honored and precious right from the start. He gave His ONLY, who was priceless and royal and worthy to be praised! That means that you are His ONLY, who is priceless, royal and worthy!

First I predicted your rescue, then I saved you and proclaimed it to the world." No foreign god has ever done this. "You are witnesses that I am the only God," says the Lord. "From eternity to eternity I am God. No one can snatch anyone out of my hand. No one can undo what I have done. **~Isaiah 43:12-13 (NKJV)**

He knew what would happen in the Garden, and yet God still chose to create us. He knew what we would choose, and yet He still chose to give us free will. And, He decided to rescue us and declare that NO ONE could snatch us from His hand. He even knew that we would question Him.

How terrible it would be if a newborn baby said to its father, 'Why was I born?' or if it said to its mother, 'Why did you make me this way?' I am the one who made the earth and created people to live on it. With my hands I stretched out the heavens. All the stars are at my command. I will raise up Cyrus to fulfill my righteous purpose, and I will guide his actions. He will restore my city and free my captive people— without seeking a reward! I, the Lord of Heaven's Armies, have spoken!"~**Isaiah 45:10,12-13 (KJV)**

Why you? Because there is no one else. There was never anyone else. There was nothing else. It was always YOU. It has always been YOU. You were chosen before the first breath was breathed into the dust of the Earth and He will never change His mind. That means you are held in the highest esteem and more worthy of being used by God than you can ever think, dream, or imagine! And God, the Lord of Heaven's Armies, has spoken!

I was many years into my walk with God before I understood this. I counted myself out due to my imperfections. I felt like I didn't measure up and, therefore, was unworthy. Until one night, God woke me up with a word in my belly! I opened my eyes in the middle of the night and just felt like I needed to write. There were words within me I just had to get out.

I picked up my phone and began to type. They were coming so fast and I was so sleepy that most of the words were misspelled and looked like broken English when I finished. I went back through the collection of words, made corrections and went back to sleep. What I later learned was, God had penned my very first spoken word piece at 3AM, which was about being a diamond and not knowing it. It was called *Diamond in the Rough.* I didn't know who I was, and I thought because I was rough around the edges and had been through some rough things and made some rough decisions that, God counted me as unworthy. He penned this piece, not only to communicate to me WHO I was, but that He was going to USE ME to speak to others, using these same words, about WHO THEY ARE. God had a funny way of killing two birds with one stone! If you let Him, God will simultaneously communicate who you are TO YOU and USE YOU, because He already chose you and counted you as worthy, to show someone else who they are in Him.

SECTION 2: CONSECRATE

Accepting Who You Are in Him

This can be one of the toughest parts of the process. For most of us, it's easy to believe that God is who He says He is. I mean, He's God. He's infinite. He's omnipresent. He's omniscient. He's everything. We can't see Him or touch Him. He just is. So, we can believe. But as for you and me - that's a different story. I can see me and touch me and JUDGE me. How can I be what God says I am? How can I be WHO God says I am?

Consecrate:

To make or declare sacred; dedicate for-

mally to a religious or divine purpose.

"(Consecrate")[4]

"Be ye holy, for I am holy." I Peter 1:15 (KJV) "But now you must be holy in everything you do, just as God who chose you is holy." ~ **1 Peter 1:15 (NLT)**

A fundamental part of operating effectively as a Kingdom Multi-hyphenate is declaring, accepting, and believing that everything you do and every gift you have is holy. Everything we do must be dedicated to the Lord for His purpose.

Chapter 3 - PURPOSE

Purpose is a tricky thing in the Kingdom of God. It's one of those buzzwords. It's the thing that everyone is running after, but seems ever elusive. As soon as you think you know what your purpose is, you feel pulled to something else. At least that's my story. The more people I talk to, the more it looks like that process is more common than I thought. It's like, the closer I felt to really finding my purpose, the further away I seemed to be called to move. Then the process seems to start all over again.

I remember telling God, "Man, I feel like I'm all over the place." Pastor Powe was teaching about having deep roots and I just felt like I wasn't rooted anywhere. I felt like I was just going from one thing to the next. I felt like I had no purpose or purpose was eluding me. I kept moving though. Why? Because when I was making those statements and asking God those questions, His response to me was, "You're rooted in me; you go where I say go. You do what I say do, and that is sufficient." What do you say to that? You just keep moving and hope your understanding will eventually catch up with your movement.

And, one day, my understanding did, in fact, catch up with my movement. It was a few years later, but it was happening! As I was working one day, I had my headphones on, listening to a message by Bishop Jakes. I do not remember what the message was or the date of the message. But I do remember he kept talking about God's glory and God getting the glory out of our lives. I don't know about you, but I can be listening to a message, listening to someone teach or preach, and while they're teaching and preaching, the Holy Spirit is all the while talking to me. I hear them, but I really hear Him talking to me, essentially riding the waves of the words that they speak. The Holy Spirit began to speak to me as Bishop Jakes was speaking. All I kept hearing was:

God's glory or nothing else.

God's glory or nothing else.

God's glory or nothing else.

Over and over and over again, it rang in my spirit as he was teaching. I said to myself, "I need this. I need this written down. I need to look at this every day." I reached out to a good friend of mine who is an artist (shoutout to Luwarner), and I told her, "I need you to paint this for me. I need you to paint this for me so that I can hang it on my wall and look at it every day." See, one of the things that I believe in is surrounding myself with things that remind me of who God says I am. She created a piece of art for me to hang on my wall at work that would do just that.

God was saying to me that He wants to get all the glory. It's His glory or nothing else. Nothing else matters if He's not getting the glory out of the things I do; out of this life I live; out of the words I speak; out of the actions I take. His glory or nothing else.

One day, maybe the next summer, we had a series of classes at church called *Summer of Stability*. I was asked to teach a session during the class on Purpose. The Lord began to talk to me about glory once again, as well as the various hats I wear and gifts I operate in. I was busy taking notes on everything the Lord was speaking to me about in preparation for this class. I was studying and doing everything I typically do to get ready for an assignment. I was also attending the other class sessions.

This was a six-week class, with sessions every Saturday, each led by a different instructor. Pastor Lamar, one of our campus pastors, was on deck to teach the session just before mine. He said that as Believers, we have one singular purpose: to bring God glory.

As he taught, everything in me was jumping with excitement. It was like my 'Mary' had met his 'Elizabeth,' and our babies were leaping. I felt like God was creating a full-circle moment for me, where all the breadcrumbs He had been dropping over the course of several years were leading to this particular moment. It was time for me to fully realize and understand what God had been trying to show me all this time.

Now, one of the proverbs that I love is, "When the student is ready, the teacher will appear." I believe that I, the student, was finally ready because the teacher had indeed appeared. The light shade had completely come off the light stand, and I could see everything that God had been saying to me about what I had been experiencing all these years.

[10] God has given each of you a gift from his great variety of spiritual gifts. **Use them well** *to serve one another. [11] Do you have the gift of speaking? Then speak as though God himself were speaking through you. Do you have the gift of helping others? Do it with all the strength and*

energy that God supplies. **Then everything you do will bring glory to God through Jesus Christ. All glory and power to him forever and ever!** *Amen.* ~ 1 **Peter 4:10-11 (NLT)**

God has endowed us with so many gifts. Often, when we see the phrase spiritual gifts, we limit those to the gift of prophesying or speaking in tongues - things that we deem as spiritual, things that we deem as unexplainable, that are easy for us to denote as spiritual. However, I invite you to consider that any gift God has given you is indeed spiritual. He is a spiritual being, and He is indeed supernatural, so anything He has endowed you to do, not in your own strength but in His, is indeed a spiritual gift. He desires for us to give all those things back to Him so that He and He alone may get the glory out of them. If we write, if we paint, if we sing, if we serve, if we help, if we dance, He should get the glory. If we design, if we act, if we direct, if we conduct, if we play, He should get the glory.

Chapter 4 - USE THEM WELL

Once we realize that all gifts from God are spiritual, we have to choose to use them. This too, becomes a point of contention for many Believers. We often hesitate or delay using our gifts, sometimes waiting for permission from someone or waiting to feel like we really know what we're doing. However, scripture is laced with parables to drive home the point that we have to use our gifts. It is imperative. We have to use what's in our hands.

We've all heard or read most of these stories before. Here, we'll look at a few of the ones the Holy Spirit highlighted for me. I invite you to really read them with fresh eyes to see them in a different light as it relates to your assignment as a Kingdom Multi-hyphenate. Remember, a story or parable, like those used by Jesus, aims to explain a fundamental Kingdom principle using something easily understandable.

Talents

In the story of the five talents, which is about money on the surface, the one who hid his talent and did nothing with it was called a **useless servant**.

Matthew 25:14-30 (NLT) [14] *"Again, the Kingdom of Heaven can be illustrated by the story of a man going on a long trip. He called together his servants and entrusted his money to them while he was gone. [15] He gave five bags of silver to one, two bags of silver to another, and one bag of silver to the last—dividing it in proportion to their abilities. He then left on his trip. [16] "The servant who received the five bags of silver began to invest the money and earned five more. [17] The servant with two bags of silver also went to work and earned two more. [18] But the servant who received the one bag of silver dug a hole in the ground and hid the master's money. [19] "After a long time their master returned from his trip and called them to give an account of how they had used his money. [20] The servant to whom he had entrusted the five bags of silver came forward with five more and said, 'Master, you gave me five bags of silver to invest, and I have earned five more.' [21] "The master was full of praise. 'Well done, my good and faithful servant. You have been faithful in handling this small amount, so now I will give you many more responsibilities. Let's celebrate together!' [22] "The servant who had received the two bags of silver came forward and said, 'Master, you gave me two bags of silver to invest, and I have earned two more.' [23] "The master said, 'Well done, my good and faithful servant. You have been faithful in handling this small amount, so now I will give you many more responsibilities. Let's celebrate together!' [24] "Then the servant with the one bag of silver came and said, 'Master, I knew you were a harsh man, harvesting crops you didn't plant and gathering crops you didn't cultivate. [25] I was afraid I would lose your money, so I hid it in the earth. Look, here is your money back.' [26] "But the master replied, 'You wicked and lazy servant! If you knew I harvested crops I didn't plant and gathered crops I*

didn't cultivate, [27] why didn't you deposit my money in the bank? At least I could have gotten some interest on it.' [28] "Then he ordered, *'Take the money from this servant, and give it to the one with the ten bags of silver. [29] To those who use well what they are given, even more will be given, and they will have an abundance. But from those who do nothing, even what little they have will be taken away. [30] Now throw this* **useless servant** *into outer darkness, where there will be weeping and gnashing of teeth.'*

Arrows

In the story of the arrows, which, on the surface, is about winning territory, the man of God is angry with the leader who did not hit the ground as many times as possible with the gifts given, thereby **limiting the number of victories possible**.

2 Kings 13:15-19 (NLT) *[15] Elisha told him, "Get a bow and some arrows." And the king did as he was told. [16] Elisha told him, "Put your hand on the bow," and Elisha laid his own hands on the king's hands. [17] Then he commanded, "Open that eastern window," and he opened it. Then he said, "Shoot!" So he shot an arrow. Elisha proclaimed, "This is the Lord's arrow, an arrow of victory over Aram, for you will completely conquer the Arameans at Aphek." [18] Then he said, "Now pick up the other arrows and strike them against the ground." So the king picked them up and struck the ground three times. [19] But the man of God was angry with him. "You should have struck the ground five or six times!" he exclaimed. "Then you would have beaten Aram until it was entirely destroyed.* **Now you will be victorious only three times.**"

Cruz of Oil

In the story about the cruz of oil, which, on the surface, is about provision and nourishment, the Prophet declares that when you use what you have for Him, **the oil will always flow**, and **e will make intercession** for you!

1 Kings 17:8-10, 12-24(NLT) *[8] Then the Lord said to Elijah, [9] "Go and live in the village of Zarephath, near the city of Sidon. I have instructed a widow there to feed you." [10] So he went to Zarephath. As he arrived at the gates of the village, he saw a widow gathering sticks, and he asked her, "Would you please bring me a little water in a cup?" [12] But she said, "I swear by the Lord your God that I don't have a single piece of bread in the house. And I have only a handful of flour left in the jar and a little cooking oil in the bottom of the jug. I was just gathering a few sticks to cook this last meal, and then my son and I will die." [13] But Elijah said to her, "Don't be afraid! Go ahead and do just what you've said, but make a little bread for me first. Then use what's left to prepare a meal for yourself and your son. [14] For this is what the Lord, the God of Israel, says:* **There will always be flour and olive oil left in your containers** *until the time when the Lord sends rain and the crops grow again!" [15] So she did as Elijah said, and she and Elijah and her family continued to eat for many days. [16] There was always enough flour and olive oil left in the containers, just as the Lord had promised through Elijah. [17] Some time later the woman's son became sick. He grew worse and worse, and finally he died. [18] Then she said to Elijah, "O man of God, what have you done to me? Have you come here to point out my sins and kill my son?" [19] But Elijah replied, "Give me your son." And he took the child's body from her arms, carried*

him up the stairs to the room where he was staying, and laid the body on his bed. [20] Then **Elijah cried out to the Lord,** *"O Lord my God, why have you brought tragedy to this widow who has opened her home to me, causing her son to die?" [21]* **And he stretched himself out over the child three times and cried out to the Lord,** *"O Lord my God, please let this child's life return to him." [22] The Lord heard Elijah's prayer, and the life of the child returned, and he revived! [23] Then Elijah brought him down from the upper room and gave him to his mother. "Look!" he said. "Your son is alive!" [24] Then the woman told Elijah, "Now I know for sure that you are a man of God, and that the Lord truly speaks through you."*

Jars

In the story about the jars, which, on the surface, is about paying your debts, the prophet tells her the **oil will keep flowing** as long as there are vessels to fill. And when she uses that **oil as a means of exchange**, her family will be taken care of for life.

2 Kings 4:1-7 (NLT) *[1] One day the widow of a member of the group of prophets came to Elisha and cried out, "My husband who served you is dead, and you know how he feared the Lord. But now a creditor has come, threatening to take my two sons as slaves." [2] "What can I do to help you?" Elisha asked. "Tell me, what do you have in the house?" "Nothing at all, except a flask of olive oil," she replied. [3] And Elisha said, "***Borrow as many empty jars as you can*** from your friends and neighbors. [4] Then go into your house with your sons and shut the door behind you. Pour olive oil from your flask into the jars, setting each*

*one aside when it is filled." [5] So she did as she was told. Her sons kept bringing jars to her, **and she filled one after another.** [6] **Soon every container was full to the brim!** "Bring me another jar," she said to one of her sons. "There aren't any more!" he told her. And then the **olive oil stopped flowing**. [7] When she told the man of God what had happened, he said to her, "**Now sell the olive oil** and pay your debts, and you and your sons can live on what is left over."*

Shunamite Woman

The story of the Shunamite Woman, which, on the surface, is about honoring your word, tells us that when we give what we have to God, He'll **breathe life into the dead things** that we desire to see live.

2 Kings 4:8-37 (NLT) *[8] One day Elisha went to the town of Shunem. A wealthy woman lived there, and she urged him to come to her home for a meal. After that, whenever he passed that way, he would stop there for something to eat. [9] She said to her husband, "I am sure this man who stops in from time to time is a holy man of God. [10] Let's build a small room for him on the roof and furnish it with a bed, a table, a chair, and a lamp. Then he will have a place to stay whenever he comes by." [11] One day Elisha returned to Shunem, and he went up to this upper room to rest. [12] He said to his servant Gehazi, "Tell the woman from Shunem I want to speak to her." When she appeared, [13] Elisha said to Gehazi, "Tell her, 'We appreciate the kind concern you have shown us. What can we do for you? Can we put in a good word for you to the king or to the commander of the army?'" "No," she replied, "my family*

takes good care of me." [14] Later Elisha asked Gehazi, "What can we do for her?" Gehazi replied, "She doesn't have a son, and her husband is an old man." [15] "Call her back again," Elisha told him. When the woman returned, Elisha said to her as she stood in the doorway, [16] "Next year at this time you will be holding a son in your arms!" "No, my lord!" she cried. "O man of God, don't deceive me and get my hopes up like that." [17] But sure enough, the woman soon became pregnant. And at that time the following year she had a son, just as Elisha had said. [18] One day when her child was older, he went out to help his father, who was working with the harvesters. [19] Suddenly he cried out, "My head hurts! My head hurts!" His father said to one of the servants, "Carry him home to his mother." [20] So the servant took him home, and his mother held him on her lap. But around noontime he died. [21] She carried him up and laid him on the bed of the man of God, then shut the door and left him there. [22] She sent a message to her husband: "Send one of the servants and a donkey so that I can hurry to the man of God and come right back." [23] "Why go today?" he asked. "It is neither a new moon festival nor a Sabbath." But she said, "It will be all right." [24] So she saddled the donkey and said to the servant, "Hurry! Don't slow down unless I tell you to." [25] As she approached the man of God at Mount Carmel, Elisha saw her in the distance. He said to Gehazi, "Look, the woman from Shunem is coming. [26] Run out to meet her and ask her, 'Is everything all right with you, your husband, and your child?'" "Yes," the woman told Gehazi, "everything is fine." [27] But when she came to the man of God at the mountain, she fell to the ground before him and caught hold of his feet. Gehazi began to push her away, but the man of God said, "Leave her alone. She is deeply troubled, but the Lord has not told me what it is." [28] Then she said, "Did I ask you for a son, my lord? And didn't I say, 'Don't deceive me and get my hopes up'?" [29] Then Elisha said to Gehazi, "Get ready to travel; take my staff and go! Don't talk to anyone along the way. Go quickly and lay the staff on the child's face." [30] But the boy's mother said, "As surely as the Lord lives and you yourself live, I won't go home unless you go with me." So Elisha returned with her. [31] Gehazi hurried on ahead and laid the staff on the child's face, but nothing happened. There was no sign of life. He returned to meet Elisha and told him, "The child is still dead." [32] When Elisha arrived, the child was indeed dead, lying there on the *prophet's bed. [33] He went in alone and shut the door behind him and prayed to the Lord. [34]* **Then he lay down on the child's body, placing his mouth on the child's mouth, his eyes on the child's eyes, and his hands on the child's hands.** *And as he stretched out on him, the child's body began to grow warm again! [35] Elisha got up, walked back and forth across the room once, and then stretched himself out again on the child. This time the boy sneezed seven times and opened his eyes! [36] Then Elisha summoned Gehazi. "Call the child's mother!" he said. And when she came in, Elisha said, "Here, take your son!" [37] She fell at his feet and bowed before him, overwhelmed with gratitude. Then she took her son in her arms and carried him downstairs.*

When we use our gifts, everything that's on God's heart AND ours will be attended to. Every use is another seed we get to sow and, according to the parable of seed, time, and harvest, the harvest time will come!

You must understand this fundamental truth about who you are. Your purpose is singular. My purpose is singular - that God gets the glory! My only desire is that He gets the glory out of this project and that He gets the glory out of you, the reader, who ultimately is designed to draw all men to Jesus so that they may be saved. That glory is meant to introduce someone to a new facet of Jesus. That glory is to allow someone to see Him as good and kind and loving and caring and more than enough. See the good work that God is doing and has been doing in your life and through your life, and lean into all that He has called you to be. Every one of your gifts is necessary. Every one of your gifts is good. Every one of your gifts is for His glory and I pray that you will be stirred up to operate and walk in each and every one of them without fear or hesitation. The time is NOW, and it has always been NOW!

SECTION 3: DEMONSTRATE

Putting Feet to Your Faith Because of Him

Demonstrate is defined as clearly showing the existence or truth of (something) by giving proof or evidence; giving a practical exhibition and explanation of how something is done.

Demonstrate:

Clearly showing the existence or truth of

(something) by providing proof or evidence.

("Demonstrate")[5]

This is where things get "interesting." We all know that the Bible says, "Faith without works is dead." We've been taught that faith is an action word. We move from a place of faith in the finished works of Jesus Christ. In other words, the action we take must line up with the faith in Jesus that we claim. Well, the Bible also tells us that God has chosen the foolish things to confound the wise. The NLT version says:

Instead, God chose things the world considers foolish in order to shame those who think they are wise. And he chose things that are powerless to shame those who are powerful. ~ **1 Corinthians 1:27 (NLT)**

This means, if God has chosen us to clearly show, or demonstrate, His existence and the truth of His Word, to be the proof or evidence, presented as a practical exhibition of how He works, then our presence will look crazy to others! And guess what - It won't make any sense to us either! We have to get this if we are to walk boldly as a Kingdom Multi-hyphenate. We must stop trying to make it make sense. Nothing about what we do, where we do it, how we do it, or when we do it will make sense to anyone, including us.

That also means that action might not actually look like action. Again, it won't make sense. Doing something, may not actually look like doing something. It could mean that faith as an action, could have nothing to do with movement at all. Putting feet to our faith could look like **waiting.**

Chapter 5 - WHEN: Can I Do It All Now?

Now that we know WHAT we are supposed to be doing, WHY we are supposed to do it and we have ACCEPTED the assignment, we're ready to DO IT. We are ready to get to work! We are ready to put our hands to the plow and do all of the things, right? Woohoo!

Wait? Not yet?

Hold up. Did God just say wait? So, you mean to tell me I've finally gotten to this place, ready to become all things and do all things and God is putting a pause on it?

I know. That's how I have felt too, until the Lord began to share some things with me about His timing.

I believe that God is preparing me for what's next. If I believe that, then I must also believe that God has prepared me for what's now. What's 'now' used to be what's 'next.' That means there was a process necessary for me to complete, designed to prepare me for my now. It was the waiting period.

Many times, we hear a Word from God and we are ready to act, but that Word was the first step in preparing us; the Holy Spirit was simply showing us things to come, with the intention of giving us a framework for how to view what we are about to experience. THIS is in preparation for THAT!

Wait On The Lord

But those who wait upon God get fresh strength. They spread their wings and soar like eagles, they run and don't get tired, they walk and don't lag behind. ~ **Isaiah 40:31 (MSG)**

According to Merriam-Webster,[6] to wait is defined as:

- to remain stationary in readiness or expectation
- to look forward expectantly
- to serve at meals
- to be ready and available
- to remain temporarily neglected or unrealized

Waiting sucks. No one particularly likes to wait. No one wants to be neglected or unrealized, no matter how temporary it may be. We don't like to wait in line. We don't like to wait on the telephone. Finding a good waiter at a restaurant is even hard - whether it's the person being served or the one serving. Either way, we are generally not great at waiting. I mean, Eve did get seduced into wanting to know things NOW.

But waiting is necessary. What if those who wait on the Lord can soar because obstacles that would have been in their way were removed in the wait? What if they could run and not tire because they rested in the wait? What if they could walk and still be ahead of the pack because everyone else got tripped up by things they learned to navigate in the wait?

So yes, as a Kingdom Multi-hyphenate, waiting is necessary. Waiting prepares you for what's next. Luke 12:35-40 TPT tells us that not only are we to wait on the timing of God, but it also informs HOW we wait.

Luke 12:35-40 (TPT) *[35] "Be prepared for action at a moment's notice. [36] Be like servants anticipating their master's return from a wedding celebration. They are ready at a moment's notice to unlock and open the door for him. [37] What great joy is ahead for those who stay awake and wait for their Master's return! He himself will become their servant and wait on them. [38] He may appear at midnight or even later, but what great joy for the awakened ones whenever he comes! [39] Of course, if they knew ahead of time the hour of their master's appearing, they would be alert, just as they would be ready if they knew ahead of time that a thief was coming to break into their house. [40] So keep being*

alert and ready at all times. For I promise you that the Son of Man will surprise you and appear when you don't expect him."

He is telling us to stay ready while we wait. The question is, what does that look like?

Waiting in the Wait

Jesus is coming back. As Believers, we know that. We know He's coming back for a church without spot or wrinkle—for a people so hidden in Christ that they are blemish-free—not because they are perfect in the world's way of perfection, but because Christ is perfect, and the Father will see us through the Son.

*He did this to present her to himself as a glorious church without a spot or wrinkle or any other blemish. Instead, she will be holy and without fault. ~ **Ephesians 5:27 (NLT)***

We don't know when, but we know it's going to happen, so we wait. We are waiting for His return! Post-resurrection, we're all in the waiting period: the period between when God's contract with us was executed and when we'll reap the full benefits of said contract.

While we're waiting, we wait.

While we pause and look forward with expectation, we attend to God and others as servants, ready and available for the master's use. This is our posture while we wait.

Pause and Look Forward

Many years ago, the Lord spoke to me so clearly and told me I would work full-time in ministry. I was like, huh? Then he showed me my local church and said I'd serve the vision of my Pastor full-time. Well, it's one thing to hear the Holy Spirit say that kind of thing, however it's an entirely different thing to act on what you heard. And this word from the Lord came with instructions. He said that I had to tell my Pastor's wife. Nervous and shaking, I picked up the phone and called the church to make an appointment with Pastor Deborah.

On the day of my appointment, I could barely breathe! My mouth was dry and my hands were clammy. I was a nervous wreck! Why? Because I'm trying to figure out WHO IN THEIR RIGHT MIND walks into somebody's office to tell them that God said they are gonna hire them! Ha! I was like, this is crazy, God! But, in the words of Pastor Mike Todd, it's only crazy until it happens.

My meeting with Pastor Deborah was one of the shortest meetings I've ever had. I mustered up the boldness to say what God said, and her response was, "Mrs. Randi, if that's what God said, then that's what will be. I don't know what you'll do or when it will be, but if that's what He says, then that's what will be."

And that marked the beginning of the wait.

Oh…you thought I was gonna say, I walked out of there with a job at the church house? No ma'am, no sir! What I walked out with was a Word from God, the same one I walked in with, AND an agreement from Pastor Deborah that God's Word will come to pass. I didn't realize it at the time, but I was literally walking out Matt 18:19:

*"I also tell you this: If two of you agree here on earth concerning anything you ask, my Father in heaven will do it for you. ~ **Matthew 18:19** (NLT)*

The wait to see that Word come to pass was 4 years. During that time, I learned to trust God and take care of His people. Not just people who had ACCEPTED Him, but rather ALL the people He created. I worked as unto the Lord for almost two years as an independent agent for AFLAC, literally ministering to people with cancer policies – some for themselves and some for family members. I was a TERRIBLE sales agent, but I was a gifted encourager and prayer warrior. I'd say what God said to whoever was in front of me. I was waiting on people while I was waiting for that Word to come to pass.

For the next two years, the Lord sent me to Grow Financial Credit Union. Being there was a testimony all by itself. Remember when I said I was a TERRIBLE sales agent? I meant it! While I was a sales agent, we could no longer afford the car we previously purchased. All my husband and I kept hearing was, "there's only two things you can do with a bill: pay it or don't pay it. If you don't have it, eliminate one of those options." That was followed by hearing another story from Pastor Powe telling folks not to hide from the "snatch man" aka the repo man! We decided to voluntarily surrender our vehicle. That's a nice concise way to say we drove that car to the bank and handed them the keys before they started trying to pick it up from our house. Did I mention the bank was this very same credit union, Grow Financial? Yeah… almost two years after we literally turned in a whole car to not just a financial institution, but to THIS very same financial institution AND branch, the Lord told me to walk in the door and ask if they were hiring. A week later I was hired, with questionable credit and a repossession from them on my report. But God...

It was here that I was given another opportunity to wait while I waited. I was able to pray with people from all walks of life. I shared my testimony of victory to encourage others and let God's glory be seen. I was not ashamed of my journey. Instead, I let God use it. I let Him use what was seen as embarrassing to draw others to Him. I served the Kingdom while at work and learned how to do ministry while I worked. This was critical preparation for my time on staff at Revealing Truth Ministries. My faith was at work as I waited on others while I waited on God's Word to come to pass.

The Bear

I'm late to the party. Well, not an actual party, but I am late to the show *The Bear*.[7] If you haven't seen it, you should; it's incredible! I'm jumping in on season 3 and I'm in love!

It was something about this show that just pulled me in. It's a restaurant show. I mean at the heart of it, that's what it is, and I like a good cooking show. I don't know if it was their fast pace or their storyline, but either way, I found myself all in. The further I got into it, the more I realized that, yes, it's a restaurant show, but it's really a show about service.

So many things about the restaurant world are interesting to me. They call the time when you and I come in to eat 'service.' They use short-hand terminology in the kitchen, saying things like 'hands' and 'behind.' They pass notes in the dining room amongst one another to provide unexpected surprises to their guests. All of it is about serving well during service.

In a restaurant, while trying to get through service, there can be internal chaos, which the show does a really good job of showing. This chaos is in the kitchen and between the front-of-house and back-of-house staff. We even see chaos within the individuals themselves. You see them struggle with wondering:

- Am I enough?
- Can I handle this job?
- Do I have what it takes?
- Should I have a partner?

- Should I do it alone?
- Do I ask for help?
- Will I be misunderstood?

It is a rollercoaster ride to watch!

Anything can happen in a restaurant! I loved watching them unexpectedly change roles. There was an episode when the head chef got stuck in a freezer, and the next in command had to figure out what to do. Did they have enough people to continue service? Who could take on his role? If she moved into his role, who could take on her role? Did enough people have a variety of skills to successfully move seamlessly throughout the restaurant and fill any role that needed to be filled when the unexpected occurred?

It was tough; only a few people had a variety of skills. Most people were really good at what they did, but had no idea how to do things that the others did.

Service was able to continue because of the few who had a variety of skills. They could fill the gap. They could cover the role. Did things need to shift all across the organization? Of course! But did the shift disrupt the experience for the guests? No. Why? Because the focus remained on providing service so that the guests would want to experience their restaurant again and again and again. **That is the beauty of being a Kingdom Multi-hyphenate.** We have a variety of skills to cover a variety of roles without service, i.e., God's plan ever being disrupted.

Back-of-House vs. Front-of-House

In the restaurant world, the back-of-house is the kitchen. It is pure chaos! We love to see it though! We love to see the inner workings of the kitchen. We love to see the chefs calling out the dishes. We love to see the food cooking, hear the pots clanging, and the water rushing. We love to hear the organization and the communication in the kitchen. Often, it seems like a little army is at work back there. They have a military-like operation. Someone is in charge, and everyone else is taking orders, allowing them to stay focused on their particular task.

The kitchen is where the recipes are created, where they determine which flavors go together, and where they decide how the food will be plated. It's hot, loud, and smoky, but it's organized.

For us, back-of-house is what happens in our quiet time with God. It's what happens when we wrestle with a Truth. It's what happens when we try to determine how we respond and how we show up on behalf of God.

Do I do this or do I do that?

It can be loud. These conversations with God are where the facts of our lives bang against the Truth of the Word. The aroma of private worship and the stench of trash—all things unlike Him that make up our self-talk—intermingle in the air. It's chaos in there! We don't know if we should have one singular thing on the menu or a variety of things on the menu to suit a variety of palates.

We're trying to determine who we want to be:
Am I the girl my mama *told me* to be because she wanted me to be just like her? Or am I the girl I thought I should be as a college student because that would garner money and respect?

Do I become the girl who longs to be someone who loves well and simply serves well? And if I am her, what in the world does that look like? I don't think I've ever seen it.

What is on the menu?

What am I serving?

Who am I serving?

What roles are necessary to serve it?

In the kitchen, they yell out things like behind, corner, and hands in a kind of shorthand that everyone in the restaurant has to learn. Handles are turned at a 45° angle. Everything is placed just so. It is organized and detailed. It is disciplined. It is consistent. It is full of process and structure. When assigned a role, you play that role and no other role. You focus on that role. It doesn't mean that you don't know other roles and other positions, but your job today is that role. It requires focus and discipline to work in the kitchen. It requires the ability to follow instructions. It requires the ability to trust those that you work with.

Font-of-house is just as important. This is where everything that has been worked out and decided upon in the back-of-house is presented to a third party. Before the doors open, the silverware has been counted, the wine has been inspected, the plumbing has been fixed and the tables have been set. Flowers have been chosen, reservations have been confirmed, and the lighting has been set just so. Again, it is chaos! The guests don't know anything about the chaos in the kitchen or that a pipe burst just before they arrived, nor do they care. They just want to be served well. They just want what they want, the way they want it, when they want it. And it's the job of the wait staff and Maître 'd, or head waiter, to anticipate their needs and meet them. For us, God acts as the head waiter, anticipating the needs of those we are serving by preparing us to serve them well. And we see this play out in the show.

This is what I believe God wanted me to see as I watched. The waiting allows us to wait well. It is our preparation time to work through the chaos in our souls. It allows us to "work out our own soul's salvation," enabling us to serve well. It allows us to operate in our gifts from revelation knowledge, where the power lies. That is where the anointing lives. It's where lives can be changed as you operate in each of your giftings.

Place of Preparation

So, where do you work out your soul's salvation? Where do you get prepared? In church. Getting plugged into a ministry where you can serve prepares you to serve in the rest of the world. This is why we cannot get so comfortable where we serve. And I believe this is why we cannot forsake the assembling together of ourselves, for it is there that we motivate each other to acts of love and good works. It is there that we stimulate and incite one another to good deeds and noble activities that are useful for Kingdom business.

[24] And let us consider and give attentive, continuous care to watching over one another, studying how we may stir up (stimulate and incite) to love and helpful deeds and noble activities, [25] Not forsaking or neglecting to assemble together [as believers], as is the habit of some people, but admonishing (warning, urging, and encouraging) one another, and all the more faithfully as you see the day approaching. ~ **Hebrews 10:24-25 (AMPC)**

We are not there to be pampered. We are there to be prepared to serve a lost and dying world that needs and longs to meet Jesus. Chances are, if God has called you to a ministry, He called you there to get equipped before you ever are released to do mighty exploits on His behalf. He called you there because there is a place where the facts of your life can wrestle with the Truth of God's Word safely. He called you there to follow the instructions of the "head chef" so that you could become skilled in your area of expertise. He called you there to learn who you're serving, what you're serving, and what roles are necessary to serve it - Apostles, Prophets, Evangelists, Pastors, and Teachers. He called you there to learn that you are enough, you can handle it, and you do have what it takes in Christ. He set you right there to see that, yes, you will be mis-understood sometimes, but that's okay; you'll survive it. He set you there to learn how to ask for help when you need it, from God and from people. He called you there to learn that if you're doing it alone, you're doing it wrong, as my Pastor would say.

So, Kingdom Multi-hyphenate, the question of WHEN you get to operate in any one of your gifts out in the world depends on when He decides you have been prepared. For me, that tends to be when I've learned how to rely on Jesus and not to allow the chaos in my soul, as I wrestle internally, to interfere with the experience He has designed for that third party I'm getting ready to meet. It tends to be when I have learned to die to my flesh, not allowing the chaos within to become a stumbling block for someone coming back to Him again. That's when I hear, NOW!

Chapter 6 - WHERE: Same Cup, Different Audience

So, I have this cup. I love this cup. It's a Dr. Seuss cup. Some of you may be familiar with the Seuss book *Oh the Places You'll Go!*[8] It's a great book! This book is given to people as they transition from one place in life to another. It's given to everyone from kindergarten graduates to those donning a hood, cap and gown for their doctorate. It's given to preschoolers and med-schoolers alike. I received the book when I graduated with my master's degree from my Auntie Brenda. As you can imagine, this cup, inspired by the book, is super colorful and filled with imaginative Seuss characters. It's definitely an eye-catching cup. And while it is beautiful, I didn't buy it because of its aesthetics. I bought it because of the message. The cup reads: "There is fun to be done. There are points to be scored. There are games to be won and the magical things you do with that ball will make you the winningest winner of all."[8]

The ball that Seuss is referencing is your life.

I believe that everything speaks! When I first saw the cup in the store it began to speak to me. I already knew that the ball was a metaphor for life, so as I read the excerpt on this cup, all I could hear God saying was, "Yes! There is so much fun to be had, points to be scored, and games to be won; there are so many magical things that you can do with this life of yours, Randi. Don't forget that!" Every time I take a sip out of this cup, I am reminded of all the possibilities that lie ahead of me. I am reminded that this life is indeed beautiful and wonderful and anything, in fact all things, are possible to those who believe. I am reminded that there is fun to be had, so have it; there are games to be won, so play them; there are points to be scored, so score them! I am reminded to LIVE! I am reminded that God gave us all things to richly enjoy! I am reminded that life is choice-driven, meaning I get to choose how I show up and how I engage with the world. I get to choose what I do with this one life. I get to choose if I live it full-out or if I shrink and play it safe. I get to choose if I show up for the game. I get to choose every day!

Well, because this cup was so pretty, it was a Seuss cup after all, it was eye-catching. People would often make comments or ask questions about the cup. With every comment, I would get to tell the story about why I have the cup. And, by telling the story, I would get the opportunity to encourage people to live this life boldly and wondrously, to be open to the possibilities that this life lies before us. I would get the opportunity to encourage people to do all of the things that God has placed on their hearts because they get to choose what to do with this life. Oh, the places they'll go!

Did I mention that this was my favorite cup? It is my absolute favorite. I take it everywhere with me. I drink out of it every day. And like most things, if we use them every day, they will eventually become tattered and fade. My cup was no different. What was once colorful, vibrant, and filled with imaginative characters was a blank canvas of stainless steel. The quote was no longer quoting. There was not even a remnant of the beauty or the message visible to anyone else. One day, I was drinking out of my cup, minding my own business, when I heard the Lord tell me to get a new cup.

The nerve of you!

That was literally how I felt and the message that the expression on my face conveyed.

I love this cup.

Now, you have to realize the additional reason why I bought this particular cup; I really was looking for a cup that functioned in a particular way. I drink slowly. I am not one of those who takes big gulps and guzzles their beverages. I drink my coffee slowly and I tend to drink my water even slower. I can have coffee in my cup for hours! I mean, don't get me wrong, I love coffee, however I'm a sipper. Also, I'm not an iced coffee drinker, which means I do not particularly care for my coffee to be cold or at room temperature. I like my coffee hot. This creates a problem when you are a sipper. So, I needed a cup that would keep my coffee hot for an extended period of time and would keep my ice water cold for an extended period.

This cup got the job done! It checked all the boxes.

So, fast-forward to God telling me to get a new cup. This cup was still doing what I needed it to do. It was keeping the hot stuff hot for extended periods of time and keeping the cold stuff cold for extended periods of time. It was doing all the things the cup needed to do, or at least that's what I thought.

Every day, I wash my cup, fill it up, go to work, drink my coffee, rinse it out, fill it with water, and repeat.

For several weeks, I continued with my usual routine. Every day, the Lord would say, "Get a new cup." Every day, I would have an internal temper tantrum because I loved my cup.

Until one day, I could not take the non-stop urging of the Lord to get a new cup. I went on Amazon and searched for another cup. I was hoping that I would find one just like this one. However, I wasn't totally sure about it because the one I have, I found during graduation season at my neighborhood Walgreens (you know how random graduation items can be at Walgreens). I really didn't know if I would find one. But, Amazon had a stainless steel *"Oh the Places You'll Go"* Dr. Seuss Tervis cup!

I bought it and awaited the arrival of my Prime item. When it came, I took it out of the box and set it on the counter next to my old faithful. This new cup was just as pretty, vibrant, colorful, and playful, filled with imaginative Seuss characters, as the original was in its former glory. As I stood there looking at the two cups, I heard the Lord say, "Different cup, Same message."

Immediately I knew what the Lord was saying to me. I knew that I wasn't having as many conversations about the message on the cup because the message was no longer visible. No one besides me knew what the message on the cup was and what it meant to me. **Yes, the cup was functioning properly for my beverage, but it was not functioning properly for my ministry.** It was doing what the cup was supposed to do, but it was not a tool to do what I was supposed to do. The cup was no longer creating doors of opportunity to talk about the Lord. It was no longer a conversation starter. It no longer created ministry moments. The Lord had given me a cup that would serve my purpose and would serve His. So, when it ceased to serve His purpose, I needed to get a new cup. Different cup, same message.

During this point in my life, God was opening up unusual doors for me that I initially was hesitant to walk through, much like I was hesitant to buy this new cup. Walking through those doors was disrupting life as I knew it. It was creating waves with people I loved and people who I did ministry with simply because they didn't understand what God was telling me to do. I didn't understand it all either, but I was walking through those doors, even if it was shaking things up in my comfortable life. On one of those unusual assignments, I was sitting on my Auntie Gina's porch, looking at the mountains across the Colorado skyline, sipping coffee out of my new cup while reading a book by Sarah Jakes Roberts called *"Don't Settle for Safe"* when the Lord said, "Oh the places you'll go, Randi, if you don't settle for safe!"

It was at that moment everything began to make sense to me. I could see all of the pieces of my life flying together like the opening credits of a 3D movie.

Different Cup, Same Message.

Oh, the places you'll go if you don't settle for safe. This is when the Lord began to give me understanding. The Bible says your gift will make room for you and bring you before great men.

A man's gift maketh room for him, And bringeth him before great men.
~Proverbs 18:16(KJV)

And where are these great men? EVERYWHERE! They are in churches, theaters, cafes, at poetry slams, workshops, book launch events, fitness classes, birthday parties, business launches and stadiums. They are everywhere! The harvest is plentiful, but, according to the Word, the laborers are few.

Your gift, given by the Holy Spirit who is the gift, made space for you in a room with great people whose heart God desires to capture. You were gifted so that God Himself, through you, could gain access to those great men! Your gift is the access pass to the room. Your gift is the key card to the room. Your gift will get you in the room. The more gifts you have, the more keys you have. The more keys you have, the more rooms you can gain entry into for His glory. He is the master key and, if we are made in His image then we have access to the master key. We only have to be willing and available to become whatever key is necessary to reach the great men He is after.

My beloved Seuss cup is simply a vehicle to transport my beverage and the "oh the places you'll go" message from one place to another. Just like my cup, every gift is a vehicle to transport His message, the same message, to a different group of great men. Each gift gives you access to a different room and a different group of people.

I came to realize that my simple, but powerful prayer, "whatever you want, God" put me in a position to become a myriad of things, gaining access into a myriad of rooms. As a poet, I reach a different audience than I reach as a singer. There's a different audience to reach as an actor in theater. There's a different audience to reach as a host for special events. I carry the same message, that a life lived boldly for Jesus is filled with love, peace and joy, in a different cup.

As a multi-hyphenate in the Kingdom of God, know this: each one of your gifts was given to you to gain entry into a new room. He wants His glory to be seen in the room. He wants His glory to fill the room. He wants His glory to be present for these great men, women and children that He loves.

Embrace the variety of giftings you currently walk in and prepare to discover more. What I've come to learn is that when God knows He can trust you in any room, He'll begin to qualify you, giving you the keys to walk into every room.

Chapter 7 - WHO: A Who, Not A What

The Bible tells us to go out into all the nations and make disciples of men. The Message version reads:

Jesus, undeterred, went right ahead and gave His charge: God authorized and commanded me to commission you: Go out and train everyone you meet, far and near, in this way of life, marking them by baptism in the threefold name: Father, Son, and Holy Spirit. Then instruct them in the practice of all I have commanded you. I'll be with you as you do this, day after day after day, right up to the end of the age. ~ **Matthew 28:18-20 (MSG)**

It also tells us the harvest is plentiful, but the laborers are few.

He told them, "The harvest is plentiful, but the workers are few. Ask the Lord of the harvest, therefore, to send out workers into his harvest field." *~Luke 10:2 (NIV)*

If we are to go out into all the earth, knowing that the great men are everywhere and there's a great harvest, but very few people to labor and work that harvest, then we must conclude that you and I have to go to more than one place. We must conclude that the only reason that we are in those places is for somebody else, or a "who." What I've come to learn is that God does not call us to a "what"; He always calls us to a "who." He may equip us with a "what," but it is for the sole purpose of a "who."

Why is this important? Because we often think our gifts are about us. They are not. Our gifts are designed to draw all men unto Him so that some may be saved. Here's the thing: your salvation is sure. It's the salvation of others that is on the line.

There is absolutely nothing you can do to separate you from the love of Jesus Christ. Nothing. Not even telling Him no about using your gifts. Once you have confessed with your mouth and believed in your heart that Jesus Christ is the Son of God, that He died on the cross, rose again, and is seated on the right hand of the Father making intercession for you, your salvation is sure. There is nothing the enemy can do about it.

So, what can he do? Distract you. He can make you think the turmoil you are experiencing, the doubt you are encountering, the indecision you are facing, is about you, or worse yet, is about your salvation. He can make you think the questions you have about your qualifications, your calling, and your worthiness are about whether or not God still loves you. He can make you think it is about whether or not God still chooses you, whether or not you are good enough for the God you serve. The fact is, all of those thoughts are lies.

It makes sense they are lies; satan, the enemy, is the father of all lies. The truth is not in him. It is not near him or around him. It is not possible for him to tell the truth. He doesn't want you to know what he's after. He is after all of those who are connected to your YES. He is after all of those on the other side of your gift; those lives who have yet to confess Jesus Christ as their Lord and Savior. He does not want God's Kingdom to grow. He does not want all men to be drawn unto God. He does not want us, the Church, to be without spot or wrinkle. He does not want that Word to come to pass, so he lies.

Your gift is not about you. Your gift is about multiplying the Kingdom. It's about adding to the Kingdom. It's about using as many arrows in your quiver as possible for the Master's goodwill and pleasure. It's about being an instrument for Him; a vessel ready to be used anytime and anywhere for anyone to come to know Christ. It is about staying ready for His glory!

I believe in the great commission. I believe God can use whoever He wants, whenever He wants to do whatever He wants to draw whoever He wants. It's His good will and pleasure to do so. And, here's the thing: as a Kingdom Multi-hyphenate, as a creative in the Kingdom, as a Disciple of Christ, we should want to be a part of what God is doing. That means not limiting how God can use us or where God can send us. That ultimately means becoming an unlimited resource for God. Take the limits off! There is a "who" on the other side of your willingness to be used by God that is waiting to meet Him. The whole Earth is groaning! The whole Earth is waiting for someone to show up and introduce them to the water they have been thirsty for.

The Bible is a series of stories to show us more about the character of God. It shows us more about who He is and who we are in Him. We know when Jesus walked the earth, He spoke in parables. If He communicated in parables with us, then perhaps the Bible, these series of stories, is all one parable. Perhaps nothing we read is quite as it appears.

We have to ask ourselves what does God treasure most? And the answer is found in scripture. In Matthew 6:21, *Jesus says, wherever your treasure is, there the desires of your heart will also be.* He goes on to say:

Matthew 6:25-26 (NIV) *[25] That is why I tell you not to worry about everyday life—whether you have enough food and drink, or enough clothes to wear. Isn't life more than food, and your body more than clothing? [26] Look at the birds. They don't plant or harvest or store food in barns, for your heavenly Father feeds them. And aren't you **far more valuable to him** than they are?*

He treasures people. Therefore, His heart is always for people, and His thoughts are always about people.

The parable about talents being multiplied is not just about money, but it's about people. The jars are about people. The arrows are about people. Seed, time and harvest is all about people. A great man I once knew by the name of Willie Hill would say, "If it's true anywhere, it must be true everywhere," which means that the principles of the Bible will indeed work everywhere. They will work in our finances. They will work in our health. They will work in our families. They will work on our jobs. They will work everywhere. The principles will work in every area of our lives. Why? Because He cares for us and wants to do us good and make us happy. And He cannot lie. If He said it would work, it must work. However, the primary reason for any of the principles to be engaged is for Kingdom business.

Matthew 6:33 (NIV) tells us to:

[33] Seek the Kingdom of God above all else, and live righteously, and he will give you everything you need.

The only business of the Kingdom is to draw all men unto Him so that they may be saved. God wants to add to His Kingdom daily. But, He can't do that without you and me, which is why He has endowed us with gifts. He wants to put us in rooms with people who don't know Him but need to know Him; with people who want to know Him but aren't sure that they can know Him; with people who have been hurt and broken and are insecure and thirsty. Will you be willing to go into those rooms to show them the Way to the well that won't run dry? Are you willing to be a resource for God to show them, introduce them, and point them towards the true source?

Another great man I knew, Pastor Greg Powe, once said "God doesn't need your ability; He needs your availability." God is not asking for us to know everything. He is simply asking us to trust Him to teach us what we need to know for the rooms He has called us to. Someone's very life could depend on it.

Conclusion

Ministries all across the world are zeroing in on creatives. Church staff consists of more multi-hyphenates than traditional bible teachers these days. With the prevalence of social media and streaming, creatives of all kinds are necessary in ministry. Services are more complex, with lights and smoke and LED walls. We're releasing music and merch. We're designing and mixing and producing and storyboarding. All at church. My own church has a vision to win back the creatives. Why is this necessary? Because God wants to use ANYTHING and EVERYTHING to reach people, including these "new" things.

The local church must have a place for us to wait while we wait - a safe space to wrestle with God and grow - while being equipped with these tools too, getting us ready to go out into all the Earth as storyboarders, LED board operators and installers, mixing techs, fashion designers, producers, and social media managers! We believe that if we limit how God can use us, then we limit who God can reach through us, and we don't want to limit God, do we? God uses these areas, too, to prepare you and me to be those things on the Earth to reach that group of people.

I believe we have thought churches were trying to keep up with culture, in an "I'm trying to be trendy" kind of way, by having these things. Perhaps, some leaders actually thought that's what they were supposed to do. They heard God tell them to install these things and to implement these things, and to do these things; they just didn't understand why. They didn't understand the purpose, and, as Dr. Myles Munroe would say, "where the purpose is unknown, abuse is inevitable."[9]

The truth is, the local church is never about keeping up with culture; it's about remaining a relevant training facility from which God's people will be dispatched. Not to be seen as relevant to the world but rather to remain a relevant tool for God's kingdom business. It seems the same. However, the nuance is very different. The motivation is different. And without that slight nuance, we become just a little off, which, as Pastor Powe would say, is still off and becoming way off over time.

Fishing was a relevant industry when Jesus walked the Earth, so Jesus was equipped to train fishermen who would operate in the fishing industry, tax collectors for the financial industry, and doctors for the healthcare industry. What is dominating now? What is relevant now? What industries do we have to STAY READY to walk into now?

My hope is that this book becomes a tool to remind you that you've been **EDUCATED** on His plan, **CONSECRATED** for His purpose, and are ready to **DEMONSTRATE** all that He's given you for His glory.

Know this: you are not scattered. You are not doing too much. You are not all over the place. You are a strategic weapon in God's arsenal to bring His Word to pass. And He fully intends to use every talent, every jar, every arrow, and every vessel He's gathered to Himself, continuing to pour oil into each one.

Keep listening to His voice.

Keep trusting His Word.

Keep focusing on Him.

Keep moving with Him.

And ...

Write the book.

Record the podcast.

Open the orphanage.

Design the magazine.

Host the event.

Audition for the role.

Take the job.

Record the video.

Snap the picture.

Start the business.

Design the lighting.

Create the logo.

Operate the camera.

Produce the song.

Write the script.

Speak.

Draw.

Dance.

Spin.

Do it all!

For the Kingdom of Heaven is near.

About the Author

Randi J. Norman is a native Floridian who has made Tampa Bay her home for the last 19 years. At an early age, she developed a passion for service, giving to others and the arts. Whether it was through scouting or her local church, Randi always found a way to give back to her community while engaging in some artistic expression.

Randi is a proud graduate of the MBA program at Florida A&M University's School of Business & Industry, where her interest in storytelling through marketing was initiated. Over the last 20 years, she has honed her skills for written and verbal communication, as well as relationship building. As a singer, songwriter, poet, author and actor, she brings a creative eye and a knack for storytelling to every endeavor.

She is an active member of her local church, Revealing Truth Ministries, where she serves in various capacities alongside her husband, Gary Norman, II, and their two beautiful children, Leila and Gary, III (Trey).

Notes

1. Cambridge Dictionary. *"Multi-hyphenate."* Cambridge University Press. Accessed August 22, 2024. https://dictionary.cambridge.org/dictionary/english/multi-hyphenate.

2. Oxford Languages. *"Educate."* Oxford University Press. Accessed August 22, 2024. https://www.oxfordlearnersdictionaries.com/us/definition/english/educate.

3. Proverb. "A jack-of-all-trades is a master of none, but often-times better than a master of one." Sometimes attributed to William Shakespeare.

4. Oxford Languages. *"Consecrate."* Oxford University Press. Accessed August 22, 2024. Accessed August 22, 2024. https://www.oxfordlearnersdictionaries.com/us/definition/english/consecrate

5. Oxford Languages, *"Demonstrate." Oxford Learner's Dictionaries*, accessed September 3, 2024, https://www.oxfordlearnersdictionaries.com/definition/english/demonstrate.

6. Merriam-Webster. *"Wait." Merriam-Webster's Collegiate Dictionary*. 11th ed. Springfield, MA: Merriam-Webster, 2003.

7. *The Bear*. Season 3. Directed by Christopher Storer. Released on FX, 2024

8. Dr. Seuss. *Oh, the Places You'll Go!*. New York: Random House, 1990.

9. Munroe, Myles. *Understanding the Purpose and Power of Woman*. New Kensington, PA: Whitaker House, 2001.

10. The Holy Bible Amplified Version (AMP). Lockman Foundation. La Habra, CA: The Lockman Foundation, 1987; 2015.

11. The Holy Bible: King James Version (KJV). Oxford University Press, 1769.

12. The Holy Bible: The Message (MSG). Colorado Springs, CO: NavPress, 2002.

13. The Holy Bible: New King James Version (NKJV). Nashville, TN: Thomas Nelson, 1982.

14. The Holy Bible: New International Version (NIV). Grand Rapids, MI: Zondervan, 2011.

15. The Holy Bible: The Passion Translation (TPT): The New Testament with Psalms, Proverbs, and Song of Songs. Wake Forest, NC: BroadStreet Publishing, 2017.

Made in the USA
Columbia, SC
29 September 2024

42620616R00048